A Zen Life of Buddha

Rafe Martin

A Zen Life of Buddha
Rafe Martin

Published by
The Sumeru Press Inc.
PO Box 75, Manotick Main Post Office,
Manotick, ON, Canada K4M 1A2

ISBN 978-1-896559-89-6

LIBRARY AND ARCHIVES CANADA CATALOGUING IN PUBLICATION

Title: A Zen life of Buddha / Rafe Martin.
Names: Martin, Rafe, 1946- author.
Description: Includes bibliographical references.
Identifiers: Canadiana 20220415935 | ISBN 9781896559896 (softcover)
Subjects: LCSH: Gautama Buddha. | LCSH: Zen Buddhism.
Classification: LCC BQ882 .M37 2022 | DDC 294.3/927092—dc23

For more information about The Sumeru Press
visit us at *sumeru-books.com*

For the Quadruple Sangha —
and for all our many guides along the Ancient Way

Contents

I would we were all of one mind, and one mind good;
O, there were desolation of gaolers and gallowses! I
speak against my present profit, but my wish hath a
preferment in 't.

— Shakespeare, First Gaoler, Cymbeline

Where man is not, nature is barren.

— William Blake

If you just know that flame is fire,
You'll find your rice has long been cooked.

— Wu-men, Gateless Barrier, Case 7

Introduction

Roshi Philip Kapleau, author of the classic *Three Pillars of Zen* whose disciples my wife Rose and I became, used to say, "Zen is rather simple. To practice it you need only one article of belief, i.e., that the Buddha was not a fool or a liar when upon his great enlightenment he spontaneously exclaimed, 'Wonder of wonders! All beings are Buddha, fully endowed with wisdom and virtue.'"

The essence of Zen Buddhism begins here, with the ex-prince Siddhartha Gautama's historic realization or enlightenment. "Enlightenment" suggests there is something you get and that once you've gotten it, you are "enlightened", but the word "intimacy" may come closer to the truth. We gain nothing. We don't get enlightened. Rather, through attention to counting the breath, experiencing the breath, or putting our attention into a koan, we become of less interest to ourselves and, in this losing is finding. The world steps in — trees, mountains, bugs, rivers, people — and we rediscover our original, undiminished intimacy with all things. No longer strangers to this earth, to others, or to ourselves, such intimacy has healing power.

Around two thousand five hundred years ago, the Buddha revealed a path of fulfillment that unfolds where and as we are. This is the essence of the Buddha Way, of a Zen life of Buddha. To begin to walk this path, nothing more is needed than sincerity and a fundamental desire to see more clearly into who we ourselves are.

With this little book I've aimed at clarifying the central role of the Buddha's life in Zen practice, a path of practice that is becoming more Western each day. It is this foundation that makes Zen a spiritual path. The Buddha's life is where mythos, ethics, and practice unite.

This seems simple enough. However, Zen tradition itself adds an interesting complexity.

Contemporary lay Zen teacher, Yamada Koun Roshi of Sanbo Zen, (heir to Yasutani Roshi who, with his teacher, Harada Soga-ku Roshi, established the Harada-Yasutani koan line, so central to contemporary Western koan practice), wrote, in an unpublished commentary on the *Blue Cliff Record* (*Hekigan Roku*), a central Zen training text:

> The standard for all Zen persons, when we get right down to it, is Shakyamuni Buddha himself. Comparing the many masters of the past with Shakyamuni is enough to see just what level these people had arrived at in their understanding.... The sutras and Zen records contain no mention of the Buddha Shakyamuni ever striking with a stick or shouting 'Katsu!'".... Shakyamuni is forever the very model of gentleness when he appears in the koans. Consider, for example, Case 1 of the *Book of Serenity*, "The World-Honored One Ascends the Rostrum": "One day the World Honored One ascended the rostrum. Manjusri struck the gavel and said, 'See clearly the Dharma-king's Dharma. The Dharma-king's Dharma is like this.' The World Honored One then descended from the rostrum."…. [in Case 65 of the *Hekigan Roku* – "A Non-Buddhist Questions the Buddha"] he reveals the Dharma in his sitting still. Shouts of "Katsu!" and blows from the stick are still all too green. They have yet to attain the behavior of the truly outstanding person.

Lama Govinda, a Westerner who, as Buddhism first made make its way into the West, committed himself fully to its practice, wrote in his classic *Foundations of Tibetan Mysticism*:

> It was only when Buddhists again began to turn more consciously towards the figure of the Buddha, whose life and deeds were the most vital expressions of his teachings, that Buddhism emerged from a number of quarreling sects as a world-religion. In the cross-fire of conflicting views and opinions, what greater certainty could there be than to follow the example of the Buddha? His words, according to changing times, may be interpreted in various ways: his living example, however, speaks an eternal language, which will be understood at all times, as long as there are human beings. The exalted figure of the Buddha and the profound symbolism of his real as well as his legendary life, in which his inner development is portrayed – and from which grew the immortal works of Buddhist art and literature – all of this is of infinitely greater importance to humanity than all the philosophical systems and all the abstract classifications of the *Abidharma*. Can there be a more profound demonstration of selflessness, of the Non-Ego doctrine (anatma-vada), of the Eightfold Path, of the Four Noble Truths, of the Law of Dependent Origination, enlightenment and liberation, than that of the Buddha's Way, which comprised all the heights and depths of the universe?
>
> 'Whatever is the highest perfection of the human

mind , may I realize if for the benefit of all that lives!'
This is the gist of the Bodhisattva Vow.

While not Zen, Lama Govinda strikes the same lofty note as Yamada Roshi. And, yet, noted Zen Buddhist teachers of old seem to
have taken a very different stance. Zen master Wu-men, who, around
the year 1200 ce put together another central koan training text, the
Gateless Barrier (*Wumen-kuan*, Chinese; *Mumonkan*, Japanese), bra-
zenly wrote in commenting on Case 6 of the *Gateless Barrier*, "The
Buddha Holds Up A Flower":

> Golden-faced Gautama is certainly outrageous. He
> turns the noble into the lowly, sells dog flesh advertised
> as mutton, as if it were so wonderful....
>
> If you say the True Dharma can be transmitted, the
> golden-faced old man with his loud voice deceived the
> simple villagers. If you say the True Dharma can't be
> transmitted, why did the Buddha say that he entrusted
> it to Mahakashyapa?

Lin-chi (Rinzai) who lived several hundred years before Wu-men,
is today widely remembered for proclaiming, "If you meet the Buddha,
kill him!" Another noted old teacher took down a wooden Buddha
from the altar and burned it on a cold winter night to keep himself
warm. What were these important teachers up to? Did they mean for
Zen students to ignore, belittle, or toss out the Buddha? Is this the *real*
Zen view? What is the role of the life of the Buddha in Zen practice?
What *is* the Zen view of the Buddha? Is there even such a thing?

Reading *A Zen Life of Buddha* won't give anyone a neat, one-line
answer to such questions. But by exploring the Buddha's life from

the ground of ongoing Zen practice, it might offer a glimpse or an experience of such an answer nonetheless.

I purposefully kept this book brief so it could serve as a reminder of what the core of Zen practice is about. The five Zen talks/essays (teishos) that form the book, present the five turning points of the mythos of the Buddha's life: Birth, Leaving Home, Enlightenment, Teaching, and Pari-nirvana (Death). It is no accident that these points form the basic outline of our own lives: We are born, we leave our childhood homes (literally or metaphorically), we come to some understanding that we express as our life, (the teaching need not be conscious or verbal) and, then, inevitably we, too, pass away.

This was the Buddha's life and it is our own life as well. Zen Master Hakuin, perhaps the greatest Japanese Zen teacher of the last three hundred years, concludes his *Chant in Praise of Zazen* (*Zazen Wasan*) with these words of profound intimacy – "This earth where we stand is the pure lotus land and this very body, the body of Buddha."

How can this body, so imperfect and impermanent, so committed to aging, sickness, and death be the body of Buddha? More importantly, how can we realize the meaning of these compelling words for ourselves?

To paraphrase an old teacher, to realize a life of Buddha we enter through whatever we're doing or not doing. It is not far off, not distant. While the forms that distinguish Zen as a living tradition have been moving West, Zen itself, Original Mind itself, which we, and all beings equally share has been present from the start. The Buddha's personal history was Asian but a Zen life of Buddha, where might it be found?

Rafe Jnan Martin
Endless Path Zendo
April 8, 2022

1

The Buddha's Birth

Our Story

In the city of Kapilavastu in southern Nepal, Queen Maya, wife of King Suddhodhana, had a marvelous dream. In her dream a six-tusked white elephant touched her right side with a lotus flower. She awoke in joy and told the king. The king's advisors said that the dream meant that a child would soon be born to them. Further, if the child could be kept from the painful facts of impermanence he would rise to the position of world-ruler. But if he grasped the reality of impermanence he would renounce worldly life, wealth, and king-ship, leave home, and become a fully Awakened Buddha. The King was both overjoyed and troubled. He'd long wanted an heir. A son who'd not just be his equal but would surpass him and become emperor of the world fulfilled his greatest dreams. He was determined, then, to protect his gifted child from all signs of impermanence.

Near the end of the queen's pregnancy, she set out for the home of her parents to give birth there – a tradition of the time. On the way her retinue stopped at the Lumbini Gardens. There, while standing beneath an ancient Sala tree and as a rain of blossoms fell upon her, she gave birth.

Legend holds that at that moment the air filled with scent of incense and beautiful voices began to sing in a language of delight. Emerging painlessly from his mother's right side, the baby Buddha took seven steps, lotus flowers opening beneath his feet. Devas descending from higher realms poured heavenly ambrosia over him, washing all birth impurities away. Raising one hand toward the heavens and pointing the other down toward the earth he sounded the lion's roar, proclaiming, "Above the heavens, below the heavens, I Alone am the Honored One. In this life I shall be Buddha." All suffering beings experienced freedom, joy, and peace. Prisoners, captives, and exiles found release. Hell fires ceased to burn, hungry ghosts were satisfied, animals freed of fear, and warring spirits stopped battling one another. Happiness suffused all beings. However, no one was happier than Queen Maya, seeing her long-awaited child at last. Unless it was the newborn Buddha-to-Be himself who already looked upon each deva, person, animal, tree, flower and stone, with the eye of a mother who regards her beloved only child.

This is the essence of Buddhist tradition's *legend* of the Buddha's birth, which uses the language of myth to point beyond the literal. The birth of any child is totally ordinary and, at the same time, a total miracle. How *do* two cells become a living person? How do gastrula and blastula become a being with talents, interests, features and personality? Where *does* a child come from? The birth of any one child is a mystery that affects us all, whether we consciously know it or not. Myth gives imaginative space to the uncanny ordinary reality we are actually living.

Still, in reality, babies don't talk. The Baby Buddha's profound utterance *can't* be taken literally. Fundamentalism's *reductive* literalization of myth takes us down a rigid road. So far, no Buddhist sects have sprung up arguing over what the Baby Buddha said or how many steps he took. Let's hope they never do. Yet we humans have been sadly all too willing to cling to beloved untruths and make mountains of not even molehills but anthills. Zen begins with a sense that our current story might at least be, if not untrue, then inadequate.

Roshi Kapleau used to say that to practice Zen there's not much we need to believe, except that 2500 years ago, the Buddha was neither a fool nor or a liar when, upon his great enlightenment he spontaneously exclaimed, "Wonder of wonders! All beings are Buddhas fully endowed with wisdom and virtue. Only their self-oriented delusive thinking prevents them from realizing it." We don't need to literally believe that the Buddha spoke as a newborn, or that flowers rained down from the skies, or that he took seven steps. However, is there truth in these mythic elements, nonetheless? Definitely. And while Zen practice offers us the opportunity to mature beyond beliefs and realize Original Nature or unconditioned Mind for ourselves, the Way of the Bodhisattva, or Wisdom Being, or Growing-Up Being must still begin with belief, with some basic faith that there is something beyond, yet not separate from the senses and intellect that can be realized. And with the belief, as well, that it will take work to wake to it.

However, while this sounds relatively simple, ("Hey we're all Buddhas. All we have to do is realize it!"), typically, it does not come easily. Fairy tales remind us that we may have to eat seven iron loaves and wear out seven pairs of iron shoes before we arrive at fulfillment. This is not simply advice for children. Persistence is the essence of the hero and heroine's journey. Persistence in Zen practice embodies our faith that the Buddha wasn't a fool or liar when he spoke of our birthright. He wasn't talking about something unique to Buddhists. Rather, he was telling us that there is something worth realizing at the core of this very life and, while we may have each caught glimpses of it now and then in childhood or as adults, formal practice can make its more complete realization possible.

The legendary words of the baby Buddha – "Above the Heavens, Below the Heavens, I Alone, the Only One" can be badly misunderstood. They do not present egotism or narcissism but actually just the opposite, expressing absolute humility and selflessness. A note to the classic Zen text *Blue Cliff Record* says, "An Ancient said, "A sage has no self, but there is nothing that is not his self." (Cleary p. 70). Through the Baby Buddha's legendary words, Original Enlightenment is given voice. While legend asserts that the Buddha knew this Truth at birth, history reminds us that that baby still had to grow up and become Prince Siddhartha Gautama who, heart-sick over his own first-hand experience of old age, sickness, and death, had to struggle to realize finally, fully, and consciously what he already understood at birth. Are we different? There is a Jewish legend that says that every child in the womb already knows all truth, all wisdom. At birth an angel touches the child's upper lip with its finger, leaving that indentation beneath the nose, and the child forgets it all. Our life's work is the work of overcoming that angelic touch and remembering what we once already fully knew. It is the work of making our innate wisdom conscious and mature.

Zen Master Ikkyu wrote, "When I tried to remember I always forgot. Once I forgot, I never forget." This is "right recollection" in a nutshell. With the self-preoccupied self forgotten, what we've been seeking is already here. We don't have to add a thing. With self-centeredness dropped away, we ARE home. It is a great relief. The last lines of *The Lord of the Rings* touch us deeply because they remind us of something we all know, something universal. Sam returns from seeing Frodo and Gandalf off at the Grey Havens:

And he went on, and there was a yellow light, and a fire within; and the evening meal was ready and he was

expected. And Rose drew him in, and set him in his
chair, and put little Elanor upon his lap.
He drew a breath. "Well, I'm back," he said.
— J.R.R.Tolkien, *The Return of the King*

The point of the journey is not to end up in some esoteric place, but
to come fully home. How do we do it? Zen practice says by attending
to counting this breath from one to ten, by becoming fully aware of
the breath's exhale all the way out, by sitting completely absorbed
in the koan, in the question or in "thinking not-thinking." In short,
by *practicing* is how the self is forgotten. And as we do, the world of
10,000 unique and individual things steps in and it is as if we are
born anew. This is how a Buddha is born.

Yet the Buddha's historic/legendary birth is a mystery, and presenting it as miraculous offers its own legitimate truth. Where *does* a
person who is the first to do what's never been done, someone whose
efforts ultimately influence millions of lives for the good, come from?

Buddhist tradition says that the birth of the child, Siddhartha
Gautama, was the first time *in our world cycle* that Original Realization
found its voice. (Buddhist tradition holds that there were past Buddhas on Earth before him and will be future Buddhas after him.) The
Baby Buddha, after proclaiming his selfless truth, lapsed back into
infantile smiles, tears, gurgles, laughs, and coos. When grown, as
Prince Siddhartha, after seeing signs of impermanence, he gave up
his throne, and set off into to wilderness of forests and mountains to
fulfill his deeper calling. In his complete enlightenment, all potential
powers of the mind for wisdom and compassion were, tradition holds,
opened and fulfilled. Amazingly he did this on his own. Though he
had several teachers at the start, he came to feel they did not go far
enough and so rather quickly moved on. His ongoing effort arose out

of a determination to benefit all beings. It arose out the conviction that there was something more, beyond the senses and intellect yet not separate from them. It arose out of dedication to the reality, not just the possibility of Awakening. It arose out of dismay and disillusionment, and out of grievous pain caused by errors and failures. And it arose out of lifetimes of previous effort as dramatized in the jataka tales.

Knowing from our own practice how hard it is to catch even a glimpse of realization, Prince Siddhartha's ability to accomplish the Path alone is not simply extraordinary but miraculous. His birth *is* cause for celebration. A tremendous amount of hard work was still needed before what was already in place for him was finally fully mature. Yet the essence was there, fully established with, "Above the Heavens, Below the Heavens."

This above the heavens, below the heavens is not simply some Eastern thing. The 17th century English Christian theologian and mystic, Thomas Traherne, speaking of his own childhood in his *Centuries of Meditation's* "Third Century" wrote:

> The corn was orient and immortal wheat, which never should be reaped, nor was ever sown. I thought it had stood from everlasting to everlasting. The dust and stones of the street were as precious as gold: the gates were at first the end of the world. The green trees when I saw them first through one of the gates transported and ravished me, their sweetness and unusual beauty made my heart to leap, and almost mad with ecstasy, they were such strange and wonderful things: The Men! O what venerable and reverend creatures did the aged seem! Immortal Cherubims! And young men glittering

and sparkling Angels, and maids strange seraphic pieces of life and beauty! Boys and girls tumbling in the street, and playing, were moving jewels. I knew not that they were born or should die; But all things abided eternally as they were in their proper places. Eternity was manifest in the Light of the Day, and something infinite behind everything appeared which talked with my expectation and moved my desire. The city seemed to stand in Eden, or to be built in Heaven. The streets were mine, the temple was mine, the people were mine, their clothes and gold and silver were mine, as much as their sparkling eyes, fair skins and ruddy faces. The skies were mine, and so were the sun and moon and stars, and all the World was mine; and I the only spectator and enjoyer of it. I knew no churlish proprieties, nor bounds, nor divisions: but all proprieties and divisions were mine: all treasures and the possessors of them. So that with much ado I was corrupted, and made to learn the dirty devices of this world. Which now I unlearn, and become, as it were, a little child again....

– Thomas Traherne, *Centuries, Poems, and Thanksgivings, Volume I: Introduction and Centuries*

The Buddha's birth led to a *practice* by which we can confirm the reality of these stunning words. So, each year on or around April 8th, we take a little time out of our busy schedules to honor the birth of Shakyamuni Buddha. We're grateful for the possibilities his efforts opened to us. But before we are lost in sentimentality, there's this from master Yun-men:

Yun-men...related the legend that the Buddha, immediately after his birth, with one hand pointing to heaven and the other pointing to earth, walked around in seven steps, looked at the four quarters, and declared, "Above heaven and below heaven, I alone am the Honored One."

After relating the story, Yun-men said,

If I were a witness of this scene, I would have knocked him to death at a single stroke, and given his flesh to dogs for food. This would have been some contribution to the peace and harmony of the world.
— John Wu, *The Golden Age of Zen*

Roshi Kapleau loved this quote, which reminds us that we don't need fantastic legends and images, wonderful as they are, for they, too, can bind us and trip us up. When we throw them away, we find that the Buddha was simply a person who, deeply troubled by impermanence and deeply aspiring to be of benefit to all, put his life on the line to realize truth and open a path to it for others to follow. Yun-men, 1500 years after the Buddha and 1000 years before us, wanted us to be like the Buddha and awake, not remain trapped by signs and wonders.

While myth suggests vast realities, the word "myth" itself has been popularly degraded to mean "untruth," perhaps due to a half-baked understanding that myth is not literal. Of course it's not! But that doesn't mean it's false! That would be a failure to understand that, regarded properly, myth leads us to the very door that Zen practice flings wide open, even as it speaks back from the other side of that gateless gate. All our Dharma ancestors, men and women who, troubled by impermanence and injustice had faith that there was something more, encourage us to keep going. The Way extends so endlessly that even Shakyamuni, the fully realized Buddha himself is, according to Buddhist tradition, only halfway there. Yasutani Roshi presents the core of this rather dramatically in *The Three Pillars of Zen*, stating that we fancy ourselves to be the crown of creation, yet from a Buddhist view we're only halfway between an amoeba and a full Buddha. Sobering words. Anyone who thinks they have gotten *It* and gone far enough might want to reconsider.

Yun-men's response was *his* unique way of honoring the Buddha, his way of making sure that we would honor the Buddha with actual ongoing practice-realization, not mere belief. His words are an antidote to fundamentalism. Yet to imitate Yun-men's iconoclastic Zen will itself lead us astray. Using harsh words, shouts and blows because Yun-men and others did is not Zen but only imitative wild fox slobber, a self-indulgent poison.

In our Buddha's Birth ceremony, which takes place on or near April 8th, its traditional date on the Mahayana Buddhist calendar, we honor the Buddha tenderly and traditionally with respect for the mythic import of his legend. Raising a spoon of sweet tea we pour it over our Baby Buddha, anointing and cleansing him, just like those birth-attending gods, the shining devas of 2500 years ago. And it has another purpose as well. In washing the Baby Buddha free of grime we wash our own minds free of greed, anger, and ignorance. This, too, is how a Buddha gets born!

In 2016 my wife, Rose, and I joined Sunyana Graef Roshi, the students of the Vermont Zen Center and Casa Zen, Costa Rica, and Taigen Henderson Roshi and the members of the Toronto Zen Centre, on a pilgrimage to Japan. While there we visited Entsu-ji, the training temple of the poet and Zen priest Ryokan (1758-1831), where we found a Baby Buddha with one hand raised to the heavens, one pointed down to the earth on the altar. Though we saw Buddhas in Japan that were as big as houses, glorious and golden, at Ryokan's place the Baby Buddha was about the same size as our little wooden one here at Endless Path Zendo, maybe six, eight inches high. And it was even less impressive than ours, being cast in dull black metal. It was humble and quite touching to see. Yet it stands out to me as one of the highlights of our pilgrimage.

Practicing realization is how a Buddha is born. The story of the Buddha's Birth might be based on history – or not. Regardless, it is remains a solid metaphor for our own potential. This very count, this very breath, this very koan can be our own entrance into the Lumbini Gardens, which in reality is the whole living earth.

To unpack the mythic language a bit further, we might say that whenever self-centered delusive thinking falls away, and a person awakes to the selfless reality of "Above the heavens, below the heavens," a Buddha is born. The sweet little figures of the Baby Buddha, then, are not simply sentimental mementos capable of rousing tender devotion. They also offer a highly concentrated image of actual practice-realization: with awakening a Buddha is born. In addition to pointing back into legend and history, they simultaneously touch base with the full potential of this very moment.

Baby Buddha's Awake! Rejoice!

2

Leaving Home

Our Story

At the age of 29, Prince Siddhartha, the son of King Suddhodhana and heir to his kingdom, decided to see something of ordinary life as it was lived out beyond the sheltering (and confining) walls of his palace. On the first day he went out from his palace he saw a sick person and was shocked to learn that everyone gets sick. On the next day he saw an old person and was horrified to discover that all living things grow old. On the third morning the sight of a body burning on a funeral pyre brought home the awful truth that all living beings not only sicken and age but must die. On the fourth morning he caught sight of a wandering hermit-sage or monk and realized that there was something that could be done in the face of sickness, aging, and death. That very night he left his sheltering palace forever, determined to find a solution to the anguish of conscious human life.

———

Years ago, when I drove Aitken Roshi to the airport in Honolulu to pick up his brother-in-law after his wife, Anne, had died, he told me that in Japan, karma is understood to mean, "mysterious affinities." To even brush sleeves with someone passing on the street would be traceable to an endlessly receding series of inexplicable connections. How much more so, the vastly interwoven connections we recognize as long-term relationships, marriage, children, friendships, neighbors, and work associations.

The Buddha's legendary home leaving is the culmination of such a lineage of affinities. Having been born into royalty, wealth, and privilege, he then sets out from all that to fulfill something that Buddhist tradition insists he himself set in motion ages ago – an essential Vow to realize his own nature and be of benefit to all. Ancient affinities arising from his own past thoughts and deeds, change the course of his present life. Knowing this tale of Prince Siddhartha's departure from his sheltering palace can help us find our own way when the going gets tough. We might recognize our own ripening karma at work. He sets out to resolve existential questions that bug us all: Why was I born? How can I be happy when I see suffering all around? How can I be of benefit? At some point we, too, driven by doubt or loss, or drawn forward by faith and hope, must leave our own comfort zones and head off into the unknown What then?

Legend says that before Prince Siddhartha was born, (his name means "Every Wish Fulfilled"), a sage predicted that the child was destined for greatness. If he could be kept from knowledge of the briefness of life, the traumas of loss, he would become a world ruler. If not, and the reality of impermanence became clear, he would renounce kingship and become a perfectly and fully enlightened Great Sage, a realized Buddha. The child's father Suddhodhana, a king himself, wanted to see his son become even greater than himself. Emperor of the world fit that bill. So, he made every effort to keep from the child any signs of the truth that all things must fade. Legend says that the prince grew up knowing only happiness and pleasure. But can even the most sheltered child know *only* contentment? Does the sun always shine, beloved pets never die, a chill wind never blow? Queen Maya, the boy's own mother, had died seven days after giving birth so he was raised by his maternal aunt. From the start,

Siddhartha's father was fighting the losing battle of a man taking up arms against the sea.

Eventually every comfort zone becomes a prison and even the most magnificent palace will turn into a cage. Again according to legend, at the age of twenty-nine, Prince Siddhartha Gautama decided that, for the first time, he would leave his sheltering palace to see the life of his people in his home city of Kapilavastu.... Mysterious affinities were clearly at work. His father ordered the streets swept, houses decorated, trees pruned, parks and gardens replanted. And he made it clear that whoever was old or visibly ill must be hidden away.

The gods, well aware that the time was ripe, intervened. Once Prince Siddhartha stepped from his palace of self-absorbed amusements, they made sure that he clearly saw four signs: an old person; a sick person; a dead person; and, finally, a wandering truth-seeker. Amid the king's carefully crafted illusion, reality struck. Drawing on the prince's own "mysterious affinities" – the pattern of thoughts and actions already set in place by lifetimes of previous experiences and efforts – impermanence, as well as the memory of the path leading beyond it became visible. In brief encounters taking place over a four-day span, Siddhartha's life was forever changed. Everything he'd depended on and thought of as rooted and solid, was revealed to be so much dust on the wind.

His father's efforts had backfired. The realization that all things sicken, age, and die, hit Prince Siddhartha so terribly hard precisely because he had been so thoroughly sheltered. Having grown up with the facts of impermanence in our face everyday, we've been essentially inoculated against its terrors. Unless, perhaps, something unusual hits – a life-threatening illness or a deep loss. Until then, we tend to go along more or less unconscious of the funeral pyres already burning beneath our feet. But Prince Siddhartha wore no armor of familiarity. Seeing it directly, raw, and all at once, he was shocked, and stunned. And, probably, terrified. Still, sheltered as he'd been, he didn't break. He didn't melt or turn and run back into his palace, draw the blinds, turn up the music, and seek to hide. His affinities, established by his own past actions and efforts (as shown in the jataka tales) lay elsewhere. Instead of running, he rallied. Choosing to live with newly opened eyes he refused to retreat into a shelter built on fantasy, cynicism, or hedonism. The sheltered prince became a realist.

A personal aside: in the early 1980's, I hosted and chauffeured around the noted author, Isaac Bashevis Singer, recipient of the Nobel Prize for Literature. Over vegetarian lunch – he was an ardent vegetarian, "for health reasons" is how he put it and, by that he meant the *chicken's* health – he said, "I am not a pessimist, I'm a realist." The Buddha, too, was not a pessimist but a realist. (Buddhism does not present a pessimistic view of the world. It does not say, "life is suffering." What it says is that an unexamined, unrealized life is characterized by suffering. And then it reveals the causes of anguish as well as a way – the Eightfold Path – beyond them. So, it is actually realistic and optimistic.) "When you get to heaven it will all make sense to you," was not an answer he would accept. To his newly opened eyes this smacked of a familiar sort of evasion and wish fulfillment. Instead, his question became – "Is there a path based on *facts* that lead to freedom *now*?"

With his painful experience of the Four Signs – aging, sickness, death, and a truth-seeker – Siddhartha's road to world-rule was demolished. Shocked, dismayed, and yet determined to find an answer to our common dilemma, he left home, wife, newborn son, father, foster-mother, luxuries, and attendants. Beneath his distress was hope: a sense, perhaps, that he was being pushed by circumstance onto the very road he'd been unconsciously seeking all along. As so many fairy tales put it, he was, "Going to a place he knew not, by a road he knew not of." He wasn't running away, but was trying to find that Way that would benefit all. In this he was rather like a soldier going off to fight a necessary war. He had a duty, a responsibility, a calling to fulfill. At the same time his faith in what was familiar and comfortable was shattered. He wasn't leaving home. Stripped of all he'd clung to, he no longer had a home. The home he'd known was gone.

Of course, such leaving need not be literal. Which doesn't make it a matter of grudgingly sticking around to "do one's duty." Lay Zen practice means leaving home without leaving home. What we leave is our habitual self-centeredness regarding relationships, family, meaningful work. We abandon nothing but our own dualistic habits of mind. Such home leaving is really a coming home. The Korean ex-Zen monk poet, Ko Un, has a poem that goes,

> But surely you can only come home
> if you've really left home, can't you?

In time the path of affinities reveals itself. Frodo leaves the Shire. Luke heads off with Obi Wan. The safety and security of the old homestead is gone, gone, entirely gone. Though Prince Siddhartha stood at the edge of the vast empty ground of reality, (prajna-parami-ta is the wisdom that has gone *beyond*), it would still take even him, gifted as he was, six more years of focused practice before it was clear. For now, with the loss of all he had known and believed, he enters the first gate of Noble Truth – the Gate of Anguish.

With the Four Signs, the walls that had sheltered, protected, and isolated him were smashed to rubble. There is no haven from the universal catastrophe. Illness might be prevented, and aging slowed, but all must swirl down the great drain of death. His sense of entitlement and safety is stripped away. No longer a privileged and entitled onlooker, he's as exposed and vulnerable as everyone elseand finds he's been living a painted dream.

This painful stripping of childish certainties is not unique. At some point we each have our own insight into the devastation. Thinking that disillusionment is the final truth, some become stuck there, settling for cynicism or hedonism. Others seek a refuge in distraction. One wonders how much of the Gross National Product is simply the result of a mass flight from reality, driven by repressed anxieties over the truths of sickness, aging, and death. Some seek to amass not only possessions but power as their bulwark against the defeat that, deep down, we all know is heading for us with the relentless pace of the ticking clock.

Prince Siddhartha's response is different. He does not turn and run. He does not try to repress what he now knows to be true. He does not hide or attempt to build a bigger, better, more sheltering palace. He does not become enraged, taking out his despair on others. Instead, he becomes emotionally naked, letting everything he'd thought to be truly so, fall away. Experiencing anguish, the First Noble Truth, he courageously lets all he's known come to *Nothing*. It is a kind of awakening. The question of what remains when everything we've known, clung to, or believed is taken away lies at the core of religious experience and practice. Case 27 of the *Blue Cliff Record* says, "A monk asked Yun-men, 'How is it when the trees wither and the leaves fall?' Yun-men answered, 'Body exposed in the golden breeze.'" The question and its answer are both worth savoring.

When all is "Gone. Gone. Entirely gone," as the *Prajnaparamita Hridaya, Heart of Perfect Wisdom,* (aka *Heart Sutra*), says, we may find, not despair or nothingness but wisdom. And peace. Manjusri, Bodhisattva of Wisdom, the traditional bodhisattva of the Zen sitting hall (zendo), often appears with a prajna (non-dual wisdom) sword in his right hand and a lotus with a book or scroll of Perfect Wisdom on it in his left. This wisdom is not added to us, and it is not gained by effort, though its functioning can and will reveal itself over time. When the sword of ongoing practice-realization cuts through our many layers of self-centered delusion, there it simply *Is*. The moon doesn't start shining once clouds part. It's been shining all along. When the clouds of self-centered thinking are dissipated by attention to the breath, the count, the koan, reality can then appear whole, perfect, and complete as it's ever been. Still, it takes courage to face into the winds of impermanence, which, like the Big Bad Wolf are blowing down our house. This is the essence of zazen. Breath-by-breath we see into the arising and fading of all we have clung to. As we attend to the practice of this breath, this count, this koan point we find that this very arising and fading, this minute-by-minute dying, is life itself. This is home-leaving and it is liberating.

Though the dramatic tale of the Buddha's home-leaving is central to all classical accounts of his life, how realistic is it, really, that even such a sheltered prince would only see illness, old age, and death, *for the first time* at the age of twenty-nine? Is it even possible? How could he not have noticed a sick person or an aging one? What about a dead bug? Or a favorite pony that stiffened with age? Something! These kinds of elements can make the story seem childish, a fairy tale designed to appeal to the credulous and naïve.

Myth, of course, has come to mean, or can be taken to mean, something that's untrue: It's a mere "myth." But that ignores myth's much deeper meaning and purpose which, we might say, is to go as far as words can go and suggest something truer than mere fact. So, looking this again, perhaps there's nothing unusual at all in seeing *as if* for the first time. Zen mind, beginner's mind may be a cliché, but:

[31]

"Ah!" I said. "Ah!"
It was all I could say –
The cherry-flowers of Mt. Yoshino!

– Teishitsu

I see the cherry flowers that open each spring *as if* for the first time. Wonderful beginner's mind! When was it that *we* first really saw, that is, took in aging, sickness, and death? The prince's response is not simply naïve. With habitual filters removed he saw sickness, old age, and death *as if for the first time*. A haiku by Shohaku strikes this same stunned note:

A starlit night;
The sky – the size of it,
The extent of it!

To be totally struck by what is utterly familiar can be a decisive moment. Prince Siddhartha's mind was blown open, seeing afresh what had been hiding in plain sight. A crucial moment presented mythically. Dogen reminds us that to push the self forward to become one with the ten thousand things (all things – pencils, stars, trees, stones, cars, people) is called delusion. But to allow the ten thousand things to step in and realize themselves as the Self is intimacy, which is another name for enlightenment. (*Genjokoan.*) For Prince Siddhartha this was a milestone moment, a step forward along the Path of complete awakening.

When was it that we first wised-up, got slugged between the eyes by the ordinary truth that everyone gets sick? When were we gut-punched to realize that even our own cherished bodies would stiffen with age? When were we stunned, down to the ventricles of our hearts, to understand that everyone, ourselves included would die and that no amount of wealth or success could prevent it? How many times did we stroll out from our comfortable palace thinking ourselves well protected before *our* walls came crashing down? For Siddhartha, the privileged kid from the rich side of the tracks, it hit him at the age of twenty-nine, over an intense three- or four-day period. *Wham!* And it was done. Just like that.

(By the way, the fourth sign Siddhartha saw was not a Buddhist monk. There was no Buddhist Sangha at the time. He saw someone on the Way, a sage or wandering home-leaver walking with peace, dignity, even serenity. Seeing the fourth and final sign, the Buddha-to-Be realized that what he'd thought was the end of his road might only be its beginning. And it confirmed to him that it was time to go – not to run away, but to seek and find.)

It's often as teenagers that we begin to smell something's rotten, out in the big wide world we're about to enter. In traditional cultures, puberty is a time of initiation, a time to die to childish illusions and be born again as functioning adults. To live fully we must die – to all that is old, habitual, and unexamined. Zazen is our daily practice of this. Letting go of thoughts we've identified with, thoughts like "I'm in here and you're out there," letting thought sequences become porous, even transparent is a kind of dying – to old ideas, hopes, fears, and conditioning. Momentarily letting them go, we wake to what and where we are. We see the wall. "Ah, the wall." See the floor. "Ah, the grain of wood floor." We hear the *whoosh* of traffic, barking dogs, a groaning furnace, the wind blowing, the "Caw!" of a crow. Ordinary things are fresh and new *as if experienced for the first time.* So begins our path through the mental fog. Perhaps we enter a sangha, find a teacher and spiritual friends. If we're lucky we come to see what the Buddha saw. Not that everything is okay and we can just go home again, thank goodness, and forget our pain. But rather, that there is a Path that appears, indeed, can *only* appear once our old house lies in ruins.

Without a model or map, that Path can be hard to find. With it – which is in a sense what Buddhism is – a map of the Way — we begin to walk our own version of the road. It may be a long, winding, twisting road with sheer drops and fitful starts and stops. But if we keep going, keep finding our way each time we're lost, eventually what's been lost and shattered is found. And is whole. Our original home is everywhere; everywhere is home. The ancient empty house that's stood from the beginning, without walls, windows, door, roof, or floor is unbreakable. To leave or be forced from the breakable home of egotistic self-involvement is our first necessary step towards coming home to what will not collapse. What is breakable must break, so that what is unbreakable may be found. As Crazy Jane says to the Bishop in Yeats' poem of that name, "Nothing is sole or whole that has not been rent." Nothing can be whole unless it is first torn, broken, shattered.

At some point our palace walls crumble, our locked doors swing open and we, too, head out on our own into a dark night, where nothing can be known or grasped in its old, limited, self-centered way. Traveling at last out beyond the boundaries of our parents' kingdoms, we enter the primordial wilderness of forest and mountain, determined to know for ourselves what's really what. In so many ways the Buddha's story is our own. Prince Siddhartha didn't leave home to become "spiritual." It wasn't, "I've seen impermanence. Now I'm going to get enlightened." Dying to his old world, being stripped of everything he'd held dear, had to have been very hard. He was human, after all. Yet in that difficulty something unexpected was waking up. In losing his old world he re-found a road to everything he'd forgotten he'd lost.

The Four Ego-Devastating Signs helped cut the entitled prince's attachments to a fantasy realm, simultaneously releasing a felt drive toward insight and compassion. But Siddhartha, "Every Wish Fulfilled," didn't then sit down and *think* his way to liberation. He wasn't a philosopher. He was a *realizer* – someone who'd had enough and decided to do something about it. So, he set off into the wilds of actual practice.

The First Truth is "noble," not because its pain is ennobling, but because it's a first step on the journey of waking up to all the good that's already here beneath our feet. It is where Zen begins. Setting out at last on our own and going, is how we develop the strength to go all the way.

3

Enlightenment

Touching the Earth, Seeing a Star

Our Story

At the age of twenty-nine, the sheltered Prince of the Shakya Clan, Siddhartha Gautama, really saw and took in the facts of impermanence. Having seen an old man, a sick man, a dead man and, last of all a homeless truth-seeker, he was precipitated into a struggle for Truth that was to persist until Buddhahood had been attained.

Leaving the palace, he rode to the river boundary of his father's kingdom. There, at the river's edge, he severed his attachment to palace life, cutting off his long hair with a sword's stroke. Crossing the river, he left his sheltered life of luxury and ease, and disappeared alone into the forests and mountains.

He made his way to the hermitages of the two most noted religious teachers of his time. Mastering their methods, he found no lasting freedom from birth, old age, sickness, and death. He moved on to truly isolated places, places that held terror for a sheltered ex-city boy such as himself – deep forests, graveyards and charnel grounds. Forcing himself to undergo the most fearful austerities, he then reduced his intake of food until he was eating first a thousand, then a hundred, then ten, then, at last just one single sesame seed a day. His flesh withered. His eyes sank into their sockets. His hair rotted and fell out. Every rib, each bony socket and joint stood out exposed, like the wreck of a ship when the tide withdraws.

After six years of such effort, exhausted and at the point of death, he collapsed, more a skeleton wound 'round with sinews and veins than a living man.

His great effort had failed. For all his willful exertions he'd found no great truth and no release from birth, sickness, aging, and death. Now it seemed that he must die without attaining his Goal. The bitterness of that moment, after six years of unrelenting but now seemingly wasted effort, was beyond belief. And, then, right there at the dead-end limit of the ascetic path, a memory out of childhood came to mind.

He had been sitting quietly under a rose-apple tree at the annual plowing festival watching his father, Suddhodhana, the king, along with all the Shakya clan's nobles and poor-men alike plowing the earth together. He saw the earth breaking open in even, wave-like furrows; the heat shimmering up off the freshly opened soil and shining on the sweat-slick brows and straining bodies of men and oxen alike; the sun continuously flashing off the gilded traces and horns of the oxen. He heard the senseless plodding rhythm of hooves and cowbells rolling in a solemn, sea-like way, beneath the shriller shouts of the men and the whirring cries of the birds as they dove to peck at and devour the billowing hordes of insects, blind, glistening grubs, cut worms, and broken bodies of mice, which men, oxen, and plows left in their wake.

The terribly obvious laboring, devouring, suffering, and dying which went on interminably beneath all the gay, surface tinseling of the festival had broken in upon him then and weighed heavily on his mind. Seated alone beneath the sweet-smelling rose-apple tree, reflecting deeply on the scene before him, he'd then entered a profound Samadhi.

Now at the brink of death and in the depths of despair this memory returned, filling him with energy and sureness. If he had already glimpsed the Way when just a child, well fed and clothed, then mere punishment of either mind or body was pointless in terms of gaining realization. He decided to eat properly again. And then, as if in immediate response, Sujata, a maiden from a neighboring village came to offer a bowl of milk-rice. When he accepted her life-saving gift, his five fellow-ascetic disciples summarily left him, convinced that the ex-prince had abandoned his quest for Truth and resumed a worldly life.

When he had finished eating, he felt strong enough to stand and, leaning on his staff, was able to make his way to the nearby Naranjana River. He bathed there, letting the river wash away six years of accumulated dirt and filth, strangely aware again of the lilting dance of water, rock, and sand. Climbing back up onto the shore he announced, "If this is the day of my Supreme Enlightenment, may this bowl float upstream!" And he cast his empty offering bowl onto the waters.

As soon as the bowl touched the river surface it forged upstream to the whirlpool of Kala Nagaraja, the Black Snake King who dwells on the river bottom. There it whirled down into the jeweled chambers of the Naga king's palace, stopping against an endless row of such identically formed bowls. Hearing that little sound —*clink!* of bowl against bowl – the Naga King opened his eyes. Slowly he raised his ancient, hooded head and announced, "Yesterday a Buddha arose. Today, there shall be another Buddha! Svaha! Awake! Rejoice!" And swaying in that timeless shimmering light, he began to chant his songs of assurance in the Bodhisattva's triumph and victory.

Revitalized and encouraged, Siddhartha Gautama strode towards the Bodhi Tree. There in the cool soft light of the late afternoon, he met the grass-cutter, Sothiya, who offered eight bundles of grass as his sitting cushion and mat. The Future Buddha spread the grass at the base of the tree and, seating himself in the lotus posture, with his resolve deeply rooted as a mountain announced, "Though only my skin, sinews, and bones remain and my blood and flesh dry up and wither away, yet never from this seat will I stir until I have attained Full Enlightenment." And he pressed forward again in meditation.

Many visions arose, fearsome and foul as well as seductive and pleasant. All the forces of life's clinging to states of joy, comfort, and ease came swaying to him in the form of three woman; the three beautiful daughters of Mara, the Tempter. They danced before him offering exquisite pleasure and comfort, while all life's terrors, fears of death and suffering, of hells, horrors, pain, ugliness, the unknown, mobbed him shrieking of torment, deformity, of all manner of terrible and disgusting experience should he persist. Mara's army descended upon him horse headed, ten-eyed, tiger-faced, many-armed; with faces in their chests, with sharp yellow teeth and blood-dripping mouths; with spiders for hands, hissing with adders' tongues. On they came, heaving stones, knives, and spears, hurling flaming discs, mud, and filth. Screaming madly, they whirled down upon him like a flock of hunger-maddened crows, wildly striving to peck and tear the slightest scraps of nourishment from a huge smooth stone. And they could not.

Then Mara, the Tempter approached the Future Buddha, and assuming the voice of Gautama's own innerness, the habit voice of his thoughts began to question the Future Buddha with these words – "Are you sure you are the one? Sure you have this Buddha-Nature? Sure you are worthy of coming to Supreme Enlightenment today, right now? Think of it. Supreme Enlightenment! Supreme! Enlightenment!"

The Future Buddha only touched the earth lightly with his right hand and asked the earth to witness for him. And the earth replied with a hundred, a thousand, a hundred thousand thousand voices: the voices of furrows and graves; voices of youth and age, of man, woman and child; the unheeded cries of beasts; the quick, unknown silvery language of fish; the sweet twinings of plants and the warm, grey crumblings of stone. For all were one voice thundering, "He is worthy! There is not one spot on this globe where he has not offered himself totally, selflessly, through endless lifetimes to the attainment of Enlightenment and the welfare of all living beings!"

Mara and his hosts dropped their weapons and fled. His daughters prostrated and asked forgiveness. His great war-elephant, "Mountain-Girded," the lumbering vehicle of ego's prideful strength, came crashing to the ground like a heap of stones before the man seated quietly and intensely before him.

Alone beneath the Bodhi Tree the Future Buddha pressed on, endlessly on without stopping anywhere, arousing deeper and deeper practice without cease, swallowing the darkness with his own light until with the dawn, his Mind rose clear and radiant and obvious as the day-break. And when he glanced at the Morning Star he found Enlightenment itself, crying out, "Wonder of wonders! Intrinsically all living beings are Buddhas, endowed with wisdom and virtue!"

It was December 8th. He was thirty-five years of age and had broken through to what others as yet had only half-dreamed. The Path had been re-opened. The Dharma was once again accessible to the efforts of humans and devas. In the steadily rising morning light, a Supreme Buddha now sat beneath the suddenly blossoming tree.

——

The above is an edited version a somewhat fuller account of the Buddha's enlightenment I originally wrote back in 1972 or '73. Based on traditional sources, that original version is still read aloud today at all Kapleau-lineage Zen centers, temples, and zendos worldwide as part of the annual Buddha's enlightenment ceremony.

Enlightenment is both the distant goal as well as the daily beating heart of Zen. Gaining calm and experiencing peace is good. But if mindfulness and calm were all Siddhartha sought, he'd never have needed to leave home. Twenty-five hundred years ago billboards proclaiming, "Get your calm on here!" were up all over town. It wasn't enough. Having personally experienced the terrors of impermanence, seen with his own eyes the insubstantiality of every person and thing, a fire was lit in his brain, heart, and gut.

The desire to go beyond habitual limits, beyond whatever we may naively term "the world," is a universal impulse. James Stephens in *Irish Fairy Tales* wrote,

> ...if you keep on driving a pig or a story they will get at last to where you wish them to go, and the man who keeps putting one foot in front of the other will leave his home behind, and will come at last to the sea and the end of the world."
> – James Stevens, *Irish Fairy Tales*, "Mongan's Frenzy"

He's not talking – or only talking – about standing at a cliff's edge looking down at the surge and tumult of waves crashing below. The ending of the world can be right where we are. It could be while talking on the phone, sitting in the zendo, cooking a meal, brushing your teeth, or walking the dog. The Buddha left his ancient palatial home of the habitual unconscious mind and kept going on and on through dark forests and over high mountains until he came at last to the end of all that old and suffering world. What did he find? What did he see when he glanced up at the morning star? Or what *didn't* he see?

Wherever we are, whatever we may have realized or *not* realized, like the Buddha we, too, can keep going, going to the ending of the world. In *Wind, Sand, and Stars* Antoine de St. Exupéry wrote about asking a fellow mail pilot, a man whose fortitude he deeply admired, about how he'd survived a crash in the frozen heights of the Andes. His badly frost-bitten, beyond exhausted friend answered that all he knew is that whenever he came to the end of his strength, he took another step. "What saves a man," wrote St. Exupéry, "is to take a step and then another step. It is always the same step but you have to take it."

It is always the same step but you have to take it. Thinking about practicing Zen is not the same as actually doing it. Which means sitting down to it again and again everyday, not an hour one day and then nothing for the next three days. Steadiness is all. The essence as has been said of genius, is one percent inspiration, 99 percent perspiration. We do the work and, then, we keep doing the work. Kensho – intimately touching the vast, pure, infinite, empty, eternal ground of Mind, of what simply *Is* – is not the end of our road but its beginning. Opening a forgotten door, we walk through it and exclaim, "Aha! Real ground has always been beneath my feet!" And then we can continue on, knowing now where we actually stand.

In the jataka tales the Bodhisattva or, Buddha-to-Be, reveals that in those past lives he woke to selflessness, to the identity of form and emptiness and, to one degree or another to original non-dual True-Nature. But it wasn't complete. It faded or leaked, became entangled with old, self-centered ways. Though clearly milestone moments they were not yet full realization of original Buddhahood. So, wherever the Bodhisattva,* the one destined to become the Buddha of our world cycle, was born, no matter in what form or station of life, no matter what challenging issues he faced, he always chose to con-

---

* "Bodhisattva" capitalized, refers to the Buddha in a past life proceeding toward Buddhahood. Uncapitalized, "bodhisattva" refers to anyone on the path of selfless wisdom and compassion.

tinue on over the next hill, beyond the next river, through the next dark forest, across the next dry desert. Onward, further, was his nature as it is ours, which is why the Tao is called the "Way," or "Path." Practice realization is not static but a road that continues endlessly. Wherever we are now, we can always take another step. Roshi Kapleau used to say that challenges and obstacles are like hurdles that help a runner dig deeper and run faster. The key to continuing is our Vow to awake to our own nature and be of benefit to all beings, summed up in the Four Vows or, Great Vows for All, recited at the conclusion of formal periods of zazen:

> The many beings are numberless,
> I vow to free them all.
> Greed anger and ignorance rise endlessly,
> I vow abandon them all.
> Dharma Gates are countless,
> I vow to wake to them all.
> Buddha's Way is unattainable,
> I vow to embody it all.

We actualize these bodhisattva vows through steady practice. Think of it like paddling a canoe. Paddling steadily, we easily move forward. With consistency there is momentum. But if we stop, we drift, and then we have to really dig in to get moving again. Consistency is commitment. To actually do it everyday is to "take another step" and not fall into, "I sat yesterday so I can skip sitting today."

Zen Buddhism reveres the story of the Buddha's enlightenment because it so dramatically reveals our own potential, even as it reveals the determined, dedicated work that underlies all milestone experiences. And it isn't that things simply just get better and better. Roshi

Kapleau used to say, "We are always evolving and devolving according to causes and conditions." So even after lifetimes of sustained effort, in the final hours of his exertions, the ex-Prince Siddhartha Gautama, the Buddha-About-to-Be, found himself mired in despair. He was devastated to discover that his terribly willful asceticism had not clarified a thing, but only left him in a dark and useless place. And then, he lets it go. He doesn't sit there beating himself up. Upon realizing his error, he does an about-face and eats the food he's been generously offered.

And even though the ex-Prince sat and sat, in the end simply sitting and meditating wasn't enough. There had to be a trigger to his realization. It didn't come just from looking within. Looking within is the groundwork, the tilling of the soil, but is not yet Awakening. It could have been a word, a sound – anything, really – for his Mind was ripe, empty of fixed notions, assumptions, conditioned habitual limits. After a long night of focused zazen, he glanced up and saw the morning star. And suddenly, AHA! "Gone, gone, entirely gone!" That's IT! A morning star sat beneath the Bodhi tree: "Star! No me, just *Star!*"

It need not be so dramatic. A poem of Li Po's from ancient China titled, "Zazen on Ching-t'ing Mountain," goes like this:

> The birds have vanished down the sky.
> Now the last cloud drains away.
> We sit together, the mountain and me,
> until only the mountain remains.
> – Trans. by Sam Hamill, from *Crossing the Yellow*
> *River: Three Hundred Poems from the Chinese*

But before his great dropping away experience, the Buddha wasn't just squatting there like a frog on a lily pad. He was seated solidly as a mountain, rooted as a tree, absorbed in *just* this breath, alert as a cat before a mouse hole. When Mara appeared, he didn't get tangled up in his challenge, but he didn't ignore it either. When situations arise in our lives we can't go off and sit until they're gone. We need to respond, to act. It need not be a big deal. In fact, it would be wise not to make it – whatever it is – a big deal. The Buddha simply touched the Earth and asked the Earth to witness for him. He didn't try to muster up a list of excellent reasons with which to out-argue Mara and prove his worth. He did what was exactly right and, also, just enough.

There's truth in the final obstacle being self-doubt. In a sense, self-doubt is what all obstacles come down to. Self-doubt is so pervasive that even when passed on an initial koan we can fall into it. "What? Can it be? Really? That's it?" we may think as long-standing habits of mind return. It need not be an obstacle if we simply accept it as another Dharma gate we've vowed to wake to. I know a Zen teacher who, after being passed on the koan Mu, put himself back on Mu for another three years (and he was doing numerous seven-day sesshin back then) before finally accepting what he already had. Many Zen teachers when first sanctioned can go through a period of feeling like frauds even while they are teaching and guiding others well. We're all in the same boat, all members of the same one-nose, two-eye society. Legend says that even after his great enlightenment the Buddha doubted whether he could teach what he had realized, doubted whether it was something that even could be taught at all. It was so simple, immediate, and clear. Either you saw it – or you didn't. From the perspective of his opened Eye, what others were there to even teach? It wasn't until the gods stepped in again, (as they had when motivating him to leave home), reminding him of his own Bodhisattva vows, that he took up the teacher's mantle and first began to turn the Wheel of Dharma.

There are several lovely touches of myth in the story, too, like when the Buddha tosses his begging bowl onto the flowing waters and watches it forge upstream against the current, reminding us that we, too, move against the stream of thoughts, emotions, and memories in our zazen. When the Naga King raises his ancient head, we find ourselves in the inconceivability of timelessness. That little *clink* of bowl against bowl tells its own story, too, revealing that countless others have already walked this same ancient road. The legend of the Buddha's enlightenment is not just a recounting in mythic language of the Buddha's great quest, but is an encouragement to us in our own life and practice right now, today.

Buddhist tradition says that we all have the nature of Buddha, have exactly the same, vast, empty nature of endlessly creative and compassionate potential as Shakyamuni and all previous and future Buddhas. From the first we are each fully and equally endowed with limitless wisdom and virtue. And because it is *already* who we are, *if* we practice, *if* we make sincere efforts then we, too, can to one degree or another, awake to this same Original Mind.

But we will not simply float into realization. As Japanese Zen Master Ikkyu (1394-1481) said, "There is no natural Shakyamuni." In other words, though we already are it, we won't realize it without working *at* it. Here lies the paradox: if we are already It, why must we work so hard to realize what we already are?

This question obsessed Zen Master Dogen: "If, as the Buddha proclaimed upon his great realization all beings are Buddha, why did all the sages of the past have to sweat blood to know it?" Why, indeed? Dogen's anguished lack of peace forged a deep resolve that, in the end, led him to Great Peace. We, too, will not know real peace until we are willing to look directly and unflinchingly into our own un-peace and its causes. Zen says, "If you want to know gold, you must see it in the midst of fire." There is no way to leap over the difficulties and get to some idyllic place called, "enlightenment." Faith and courage may be two words, but they might mean the same thing.

Actually, enlightenment isn't even a "thing." It's not something we can get – except in the sense of, "Oh. I get it!" If anything, it comes from losing not gaining, losing all the ancient, interior, self-centered "stuff" that cuts us off and leaves us isolated and alone. With that wonderful failure, that liberating loss, we uncover our original, unblemished intimacy with sun, moon, stars, wind, rain, snow, clouds, trash, bugs, cats, rivers, mountains, trees, people, joy, and sorrow. We do not gain it, because it has never been lost. Like the ground, it has always been here. We just haven't had the steadiness to notice.

And, it's not that "I" become intimate with everything. Keizan Jokin, in the opening of the *Denkoroku, Transmission of the Light*, writes – "Shakyamuni Buddha saw the morning star and was enlightened, and he said, 'I and the great earth and beings simultaneously attain the Way.'" In his teisho (Dharma talk) on this he adds: "The so-called I is not Shakyamuni Buddha and Shakyamuni Buddha also comes from this 'I.'"

Zen says, "Okay, if we are this enlightened nature, where is it? And why don't we know it?" In zazen we bore into such questions like a thirsty person drilling for water. A sonar survey – the life of the Buddha, the Buddha's past life stories (jatakas), the sutras, Zen teaching, the life stories of our Dharma ancestors, men and women, lay and ordained shows us that all the water we will ever need is already beneath our feet. So we sit and sit. We come to sesshin, zazenkai, dokusan, and teisho, to services and ceremonies. We examine precepts, experience this breath, count this breath, sit fully, read sutras, return to koan point after koan point. In these ways we actualize our original Vow, the vow of unconditioned Mind, of all maturing-beyond-self-centeredness-wisdom beings or bodhisattvas, to abandon self-oriented dualistic thinking and realize the ancient Way for the benefit of all.

The wisdom that is compassion, the compassion that is no other than wisdom, comes down to this moment of practice. Which is easy enough to say, but what is it? I would say that the essence of continuous practice is the lessening of our unconscious, habitual identification with self-centeredness. This is the core of zazen. It is not a matter of pushing the self away or of suppressing or ignoring it, all of which only serve to reify and confirm what is not actually so. It comes from attending to this very self as it arises in all its confusion, without flinching, without evading, seeing it so clearly that we ultimately find it – wonder of wonders! – transparent and empty. "The bodhisattva of compassion from the depths of prajna wisdom saw the emptiness of all five skandhas and sundered the bonds that create suffering." This is Prajnaparamita, the perfection of highest wisdom. To paraphrase Dogen, "To study the Way is to study the self. To study the self, is to forget the self. To forget the self is to realize intimacy with all things. This selflessly intimate *practice* continues endlessly." Practice is not cast aside with realization; it *is* realization in action. Practice continues but it is no longer forced. Instead, it is simply who we are.

The Buddha, the ex-Prince, touched the Earth after lifetimes of such practice, as the past-life jataka tales show. For many of us, too, it may not be until after years of practice and various milestones that the gateless gate swings open and we truly, personally *Know*. Yet even this, overwhelming as it might be, we eventually come to see is simply another beginning, another step, not yet the end of the road at all.

The Buddha's realization points the Way. Although in substance every kensho, the small kind we're likely to realize and the Buddha's own great enlightenment are the same, in content they are vastly different. Buddhist mythos says that in this World Age no one experienced more deeply than Shakyamuni, because no one had worked so hard or so long to prepare for it. He touched not just the ground but the bottomless bottom and soaring heights. Comparing our realization of practice, our practice of realization to his would be like comparing the finger painting of a kindergartener to a work by a Rembrandt or Picasso. The substance is the same. Both are paintings. But the degree of conscious realization is vastly different.

The Buddha's story, his home-leaving and forest path exertions, his abandonment by his ascetic disciples and his solitary confrontation with Mara – the primordial force of his own habitual ignorance – completes his own practice Path of many lifetimes. Touching the Earth, he gets up and walks on, transcending the final temptation to sit forever at ease in his long-sought, hard-won pavilion of enjoyment, freedom, wisdom, and peace. Instead, he devotes his next nearly fifty years to walking the dusty roads of India, teaching those who, while in reality are just as complete and whole as he, don't yet know it. He goes back into the seeming chaos of the ten thousand things, at peace with it all, a half smile on his lips.

Just prior to the moment of enlightenment, after the Buddha-to-Be's six years of exhaustive effort, (and, according to Buddhist tradition, endless kalpas of jataka practice-exertions), going to the limit, trying and trying with all he had, drawing on the power of his own countless efforts, failures, and victories, Mara, the Buddhist Tempter or Distracter, the inner voice of ego, appears. Mara is now worried and, so, makes a final, desperate, all-out, last-ditch effort to turn the once sheltered, now deeply determined ex-prince from his Goal, by pulling out his ace in the hole – self-doubt. "What? I have this True Nature? It is *me*? And what's more I can realize it? *Really*?"

Self-doubt is so sticky, so tough to deal with because it insidiously sneaks up on us, convincing us that in reality we are what we feel ourselves to be — a small, isolated, separate, winning-losing interior self, a self that can be saved, a self that can be *enlightened.* Self-doubt glues us to the stickiness of what is only provisionally real. Obstacles and challenges can do this, too. We get caught up in our selves, in our personal histories and issues and are triggered into being defensive and reactive. We feel that we must overcome what confronts us or retreat protectively from it. This is natural. Yet if we pay attention and practice *into* the challenge, *into* the stress, something shifts, opens, and falls away.

Sometimes the deepening of practice itself can elicit the challenge. So, as the Buddha's practice deepened, Mara appeared. Confronting the Buddha-to-Be he asks, "How can you, a sheltered, entitled ex-prince, be worthy of the Supreme Goal of perfect enlightenment? Better men and women than you have tried and failed. You're young and a beginner. Give it time. You've got the basic ability but now? No way. Back off! Take it slow."

It is reasonable advice, reasonable as all get-out, devilishly reasonable. "Take it easy. Be careful. Go slow and steady. Prepare. Reduce attachments and ego-concerns. Be humble. Don't be hasty."

Such Maras or Distracters are said to exist throughout the endless worlds. The good news is that Maras may actually be advanced bodhisattvas (*The Vimalakirti Sutra* takes this radical position), whose challenges are skillful means or, upaya intended to help us mature. Now, at this crucial juncture, with worlds hanging in the balance, Mara comes to check out the ex-Prince Siddhartha and see: is he ready or not?

Siddhartha doesn't waste breath in arguing with the habit voice of his own unconscious predilection toward self-centeredness. Nor does he even try to put together a reasonable counter-argument. To enter the fray is to have already lost. "Ready? Not ready? A self that gains? A self that loses? A self that has It? A self that doesn't have It?" He doesn't get sucked into Mara's metaphor at all. Instead, he probably smiled, maybe even shook his head in pity for poor old Mara, then reached down and touched the Earth and let the humble, always present, endlessly-trod-on Earth speak for him. And the Earth replied with its thousands of living voices as One: "He is worthy!" Inter-being, to use Thich Nhat Hanh's felicitous term, awakes. Mara then gives up and turns away.

At his moment of final challenge, the Buddha touched the Earth, the ground beneath him. He didn't reach toward the sky or beg for help from above. He didn't fall for Mara's metaphor and try to win the debate or out-argue the Distracter. He simply touched the always present, selfless, sat on, trod on ground, and asked the Earth to witness for him. Her humbly solid response confirms him, overwhelming self-doubt. What builds solid ground beneath us, is the work we do now. This is where and how we touch ground. It is this breath, this count, this koan, this pain in the knee, this, "Caw!" of the crow. Roshi Kapleau used to say, "If you don't let the Dharma down, the Dharma will never let you down." He also said that no sincere effort is ever wasted. Every effort adds to our stock of merit, which one day we will draw on.

Essential nature, Mind itself, is the ground beneath us. Past thoughts, past efforts, and decisions lead effortlessly into this present moment in which we now sit, walk, stand, speak, eat, work, worry, create. Come day's end, we say "good night," and lie down on the ground we practice from, have always been on, whether we knew it or not.

Our fundamental Vow as human beings is to know ourselves. We practice not to become special this's or that's but to know who or what we already *are*. Zen Master Dogen said: "When the self advances to confirm the 10,000 things it is called delusion. When the 10,000 things advance and confirm the Self it is intimacy or enlightenment." The ten thousand things are birds, bugs, clouds, mountains, rivers, people, animals, traffic sounds, cell phones, raindrops, pebbles, clumps of earth, bright morning stars. Ordinary things confirm us, tell us, indeed, *make* us who we are, everyday. There is no barrier between us, and a single thing. Nothing is hidden. That enlightenment is intimacy is not cleverness but truth.

Because this is so, each of us already has the potential to wake to it. Touching the Earth is always possible because our real ground is never far away.

And neither is a star.

4

Teaching

Our Story

Zen is said to be a teaching not dependent on words or letters but rather one that points directly, without intermediaries, to the human Mind. So, it should come as no surprise that Zen tradition, which presents itself as the -essence of the Buddha's teaching, finds this approach already fully alive in Buddha's teaching from the start. The Buddha of Zen is the original Zen Master, who teaches by demonstrating and presenting rather than by talking "about." He offers living truth, not philosophy. Like the monk in the tenth and final Zen Oxherding picture, he enters the marketplace (the highways and byways of ordinary human life) with helping hands. Which sounds pretty good. Who doesn't need help? But what does such help look like? What kind of help does the enlightened Buddha offer?

To clarify, here's *Wu-men kuan* (*Mumonkan* in Japanese), or *Gateless Barrier*, Case 6: "The Buddha Holds Up a Flower."

> Once, in ancient times, when the World-Honored One was at Mount Grdhrakuta, [Vulture Peak, one the Buddha's favorite places for teaching. Near Rajgir or Rajagaha in Bihar, India] he held up a flower before his assembled disciples. At this all were silent. Only Mahakashyapa broke into a smile.
>
> The World-Honored One said, "I have the All-pervading Eye of the True Dharma, the Subtle Mind

of Incomparable Nirvana, the True Form of Formless Form and the Flawless Gate of the Supreme Teaching. It is not established upon words and phrases and is transmitted outside all teachings. I now entrust this to Mahakashyapa.

A tiny gesture can become a profound teaching. Seated beneath the Bodhi Tree, the Buddha touched the Earth and vanquished Mara. Here he holds up a flower and transmits the Dharma. Each slight gesture speaks volumes and has the power to transform lives.

———

After his great enlightenment, the Buddha had a choice. He could stay where he was enjoying the bliss, freedom, and insight of his attainment (and, indeed, legend says he was sorely tempted to do just that), or he could begin the profoundly absurd, even perhaps impossible task of saving the many already saved but still deluded and, so, still suffering beings.

It took him a while to resolve the challenge. After his realization he sat beneath the Bodhi tree for three weeks, emptied out, absorbed in liberation, insight, and joy. During this time a storm arose and as the newly awakened Buddha sat on unmoving, a naga (serpent) king named Muccalinda, rose up out of the Earth and spread its cobra hood over him, protecting him from wind and rain. In the midst of this great storm, the Buddha was facing a dilemma: could realization be taught? Could he or anyone teach it? It was perfectly whole from before the beginning. Everyone already had it. So, how could you teach people to attain what they already had in full? The truth while open, clear, and irrefutable, could not be mentally or conceptually grasped. Could it be pointed to? Or would others have to find their own way to where they already were, when their karma was ripe? But that would take a long time and involve much suffering. Teaching would speed things up. Still, as there was nothing to gain and from an absolute perspective, no suffering beings to gain it, why even try? What was there to say? From the start, it was done, given, accomplished. Could he now relax, live a life of joyous, unburdened ease and when the karma of this life played itself out, step forward into the completeness of pari-nirvana?

The gods who had intervened before stepped in again, reminding him that anguish was everywhere and that there were many ready to put his teaching into practice.

The image they gave him was evocative. The gods showed him a vision – this seems to be how gods speak – that living beings are like lotuses in a pond. Some are buried in the mud at the pond's bottom, some have risen from the mud into the water, others, while still beneath the surface are nearing light and air, while others still are even now opening above the water in bright sunlight. All are equally lotuses, only they are in different stages of realizing their potential.

("Buddha," by the way, has the same original root as "to bud." A Buddha is a budded being!)

Where do intuitions, promptings to do our best regardless of challenge or risk, come from? It seems instinctive for some people to respond courageously and selflessly. Abraham Lincoln spoke of the "angels of our better nature." The prompting of gods or angels seems as good a metaphor as any. Moved by such divine encouragement, then, the Buddha set off from beneath the Bodhi Tree and along the dusty roads of his native land, to teach the Dharma. While realization couldn't be taught, the Way to it could. And that he would do. And, because of his decision twenty-five hundred years ago, we have this practice, this Path, and ... this *flower*.

The Buddha must have trusted his audience and their potential when he held up that flower. Like the ringing of a bell, the taste of tea, the wetness of water, the pain of a stubbed toe there was just this ... flower! Who didn't have the eyes to see? He was "presenting the shout" – the literal meaning of "teisho" – not giving a lecture.

Still, it must have been astonishing back then, more than two thousand years ago, so long before holding up a flower had become a New Age cliché. Perhaps thousands of people had gathered and were waiting expectantly for the Buddha's profound words. Would the Great Teacher present a new sutra? Would he perform miracles? Would gods descend from the skies? Would the Master enlighten ten, a hundred, a thousand people? Anything was possible.

He did none of those things. Without explanation, he held up a flower. It was radical. Beethoven smiles and plays not a note. Shakespeare bows and walks off stage. The Buddha holds up a flower. Was there disappointment? Confusion? Nervous laughter? Were there shouts of "Charlatan!" countered by intricate defenses of the Master's great wisdom? Most likely all of that, and more.

A flower was held up and a seed was planted. Maybe some puzzled over it wondering, "Is the Buddha saying we should be like this flower? Is he telling us to live like this flower, without concerns for what is to come?" If they did, they might have benefited from such thinking. But Mahakashyapa alone just cracked up and broke into a smile. Why?

And why does Master Wu-men insist we explore this as a koan, not simply take it as an article of faith, or as a parable? As a koan it is no longer legend or history, no longer the Buddha's or Mahakashyapa's story. It steps out of history and is our own story, our own dilemma, our own truth, right now. We *realize* this flower. The story of the Buddha's enlightenment in the Soto koan collection, *Denkoroku,* (*Transmission of the Light*) comes with this verse:

> One branch from the old plum tree
> Extends splendidly forth.
> Thorns come forth at the same time.

For our present purpose we can say that the difficulty of grasping this thorny point has fortunately come down to each one of us. Without this flower there would be no zazen, no sesshin, no zazenkai, no Zen teaching, no you and me practicing. No flower, no Zen. It's that simple. Without this flower and Mahakashyapa's blossoming smile, the Buddha would have passed into his pari-nirvana and his teachings become a dusty pile of fading words. Instead, we have the living transmission of practice-realization extending through generations. Wu-men's commentary says:

> Golden-faced Gautama is certainly outrageous. He turns the noble into the lowly, sells dog flesh advertised as mutton, as if it were so wonderful.
>
> However, suppose that all the monks had smiled, how would the All-pervading Eye of the True Dharma have been transmitted? Or suppose that Mahakashyapa had not smiled, how could he have been entrusted with it?
>
> If you say the True Dharma can be transmitted, the golden-faced old man with his loud voice deceived the simple villagers. If you say the True Dharma can't be transmitted, why did the Buddha say that he entrusted it to Mahakashyapa?

Master Wu-men wants us to get clear not remain distant, vague, or abstract about the nature of realization (kensho, awakening, enlightenment, intimacy), and Dharma transmission. What is realization and what is transmission? When the "Caw!" of the crow sounds within my own heart, what "other" could there be? Selfless intimacy *is* realization. But what is transmission? Does it differ from realization? If so, how? If it didn't, then anyone with some realization should receive transmission. But that's not what happens. Many are passed on koans, some complete the entire koan curriculum, but few receive transmission. While the Buddha transmitted the All-Pervading Eye of the True Dharma to Mahakashyapa alone, didn't everyone there equally have Original Enlightenment, Original Mind? Didn't the Buddha himself proclaim this truth at the moment of his own great insight? "Wonder of wonders! All beings are Buddha!" So, why does he say that Mahakashyapa alone has it? Plus, when the All-Pervading Eye of the True Dharma was transmitted, what did Mahakashyapa actually receive?

Ananda, the Buddha's first cousin and attendant, he of perfect memory through whom the Buddha's teishos – his sutras – have come down to us, wanted to know. Having faithfully attended the Buddha for many years it's said that his great regard for the Buddha as a person kept him from awakening fully to what the Buddha taught. So, he was anxious and puzzled about this thing called "transmission." What did Mahakashyapa have or get that Ananda and others didn't? After the Buddha passed into his pari-nirvana and Mahakashyapa began leading the community, Ananda asked about it. Case 22 of the *Gateless Barrier*, "Mahakashyapa's Flagpole" goes:

Ananda asked Mahakashyapa, "The World-Honored One transmitted the golden robe to you. What else did he transmit to you?"

Mahakashyapa said, "Ananda!"

Ananda said, "Yes!"

Mahakashyapa said, "Pull down the flagpole at the gate."

Danan Henry Roshi received the Dharma from Philip Kapleau Roshi, and from Robert Aitken Roshi. He transmitted his Dharma to me, making me his heir. Does that mean our minds are telepathically linked? Do we now think the same inexpressibly lofty thoughts? What was transmitted? According to Buddhist tradition, the insight that began with Shakyamuni Buddha in this world cycle, (there are said to have been previous world cycles and previous Buddhas), was transmitted to Mahakashyapa, who transmitted it to Ananda, who likewise transmitted it on, and so on and on transmission after transmission through the past 2500 years down to us today. This is the legend and, while its truth resides in the actualities of practice-realization, the reality is complex. There was not just one line of transmission but, rather, it was like mycelium threads multiplying, spreading, overlapping, increasing in size and density outward as well as inward, realization springing up in multiples, a web of realization extending outward to the limits of each generation, a jeweled web, a fungal mat of insight absorbing and wielding together a new cultural frame, the practice forms themselves coalescing and adapting, evolving and maturing. But in essence, all of what we practice, all of how we've benefited *from* practice originates with the Buddha's Awakening and this first transmission to Mahakashyapa. In short, it comes from this flower. Yet did this moment with the flower ever really happen? Aitken Roshi asks, "Would it make a difference if the Buddha never existed? Here's his view:

True religious practice is grounded in the nonhistorical fact of essential nature. "The World Honored One Twirls a Flower," "Pai-chang's Fox," and all the other fabulous cases of Zen literature are your stories and mine, intimate accounts of our own personal nature and experience.

— Robert Aitken, *The Gateless Barrier:*
The Wu-men kuan (Mumonkan)

The flower is held up now! This is the moment in which the Buddha gives his teisho, raises a flower, and Venerable Mahakashyapa breaks into a smile. It is not far-off in time or space, not lingering back in history. And yet, though it is here now, it can take hours, weeks, years for any one of us to see it clearly enough to continue the legacy bequeathed to us by the Buddha, Mahakashyapa, Ananda and all the teachers who followed after them.

Regardless of where we may individually be at, each of us will leave our own legacy for good or ill to future generations. What shall our legacy be? Some legacies are just dust and ashes, while others remain endlessly green, capable of bringing forth new life. Ryokan, the Soto priest, poet, calligrapher, and extraordinarily humble human being wrote:

My legacy —
What will it be?
Flowers in spring,
The cuckoo in summer,
And the crimson maples
Of autumn...

In his commentary to the case, Wu-men brings us fully home. "Golden-faced Gautama is certainly outrageous. He turns the noble into the lowly, sells dog flesh advertised as mutton, as if it were so wonderful." In short, "Get down off your pedestal oh, Buddha! You're hawking cheap goods as if they were the high-class stuff. But what are you really up to with your radiant, golden face, shining like a morning star?" Then he goes on to ask what if all the monks had smiled? Would there have been transmission? And what if Mahakashyapa hadn't smiled? How would things have played out then? Can something as profound as Dharma transmission depend on such flimsy supports as a flower and a smile? Can the True Dharma be transmitted? What is it, after all, and how does it get passed on? Is there some deception at work? Is the myth a lie? Did the golden-faced old man with the loud voice deceive the simple villagers? And who are these simple villagers anyway?

Joseph Campbell pointed to myth as the highest and furthest language can go into truth. Yet, Wu-men takes pains to downplay all such profundities. "Golden-faced old man" and "simple villagers" hardly seem the stuff of legend. Maybe Wu-men's verse will help:

> Holding up a flower
> the snake shows it tail.
> Mahakashyapa breaks into a smile,
> and people and devas are at a loss.

Holding up a flower, the snake shows its tail. Hold on. Isn't a snake ALL tail? Holding up a flower, then, is the whole deal, the whole nature, the whole Mind, the entire character fully exposed. Nothing's hidden. If it's an open secret, how could there be deception? In his *Zazen Wasan, Chant in Praise of Zazen,* Master Hakuin writes:

What is there outside us?
What is there we lack?
Nirvana is openly shown to our eyes.
This Earth where we stand
Is the pure lotus land.
And this very body
The body of Buddha.

Yet, open and unhidden as it is, how hard we work at it, breath-by-breath, sitting after sitting, sesshin after sesshin, koan after koan. And, still, ITs full blossoming evades us. We keep at it yet hardly seem to have begun. It is the old paradox – if what we seek is not hidden but is right where we are, why don't we see it? Why don't we fully know it and live it, right now? Only the Venerable Mahakashyapa seems to be in on the joke. And he cracks up, breaking into that smile. Everyone else – even the devas, the gods – seem confused. Which is when Wu-men relents and offers us some relief, acknowledging that our dullness is not all that unusual. Why should we be ashamed when even arhats, bodhisattvas, and gods are thrown for a loop by a simple flower?

And, yet – there's that tail. In a different context, Case 38 of the *Gateless Barrier*, Master Wu-men writes:

This tiny little tail –
What a wonderful thing it is!

With this reference to the snake and its tail, myth slithers back in. A snake in Buddhist tradition can be a wise and powerful naga – a great serpent being. Nagas, Buddhist legends say, guard the perfect wisdom (prajnaparamita) teachings in their jeweled underwater palaces, waiting for the day when human beings will be mature enough to receive these teachings in full. So that old man, that golden-faced swindler hawking his cheap goods, in holding up a flower showed his real identity. Seeing the tail, all is instantly revealed. And, lo and behold, he's no swindler but a great, naga-like wisdom being! And that flower he's holding, why, it's actually a great treasure!

Isn't that a terrific joke? Doesn't it crack you up and just make you want to break into a smile?

5

Death

Our Story

After a lifetime of teaching, the Buddha, now eighty years of age, realized that in three months he would enter nirvana. Gathering his community, he began the long walk to Pava and the twin Sala trees in the land of the Mallas, where he meant to take his final rest. While on the way, he and his community were offered a generous meal by the smith, Cunda. At the meal the Buddha ate a dish of mushrooms or pork (unknown now) that was spoiled. Quickly he forbade anyone else to eat it and told his attendant and cousin, Ananda, that the smith was not to be blamed for what was to happen. He added that such a meal that initiates a Buddha's pari-nirvana (full entrance into nirvana) is actually a good and necessary thing. When they set off again the Buddha was in pain and when they at last arrived, he was near death. He lay down on his right side upon a stone couch between the twin Sala trees. Lying there he made his farewells, offered final guidance, resolved disciples' remaining doubts, and personally accepted one last student. Entering the dying process (pari-nirvana), fully conscious and at ease, he passed peacefully from this life. According to legend, his final instructions to his assembled followers stated:

> Liberation cannot come from mere sight of me. It demands serious efforts in spiritual practice. The sight of the physician cures no illness. One must take the medicine to be well. So be vigilant! Meditate and

discover the truth for oneself. Life is shaken by many difficulties, even as the flame of a lamp is shaken by the wind. Do good deeds and strive for realization.

His final words to his disciples went further:

> Everything comes to an end though it may last an eon. I have done all I could, have disciplined in heaven and earth all those I could discipline. I have motivated and trained them and set them in the stream that leads toward Liberation. Hereafter my Dharma shall abide for generations among living beings. Recognize the true nature of things and do not be anxious. Separation cannot be avoided. Be mindful and vigilant. The time for my entry into Nirvana has arrived.

It is said that these were his final words.

———

Let's be honest: Death is our greatest difficulty. Accepting it and, for lack of a better word, *doing* it, are our most severe challenges, fraught with deepest anxiety and trauma. All challenges and difficulties in life seem to stem from or circle around this primal one of awesome finality. A personal realization of this can be devastating. I attended my mother in her dying. She was younger then than I am now, and I was younger then than my own children are at present. Yet I can still hear her final stunned and terrified words as the reality of it hit her: "Oh, G-d," she exclaimed. "I am dying!"

To face head-on what, as Shakespeare wrote, "... ends this strange eventful history ... Sans teeth, sans eyes, sans taste, sans everything,"

(*As You Like It*), can be terribly hard. It is beyond everything and anything we can imagine. A lifetime of practicing, of learning to be fully
present with what IS, seeing through habitual, unconscious identifi-
cations with the isolated, interior, small-minded sense of ourselves
crouched down and terrified, is our best preparation. Roshi Kapleau
liked Woody Allen's joke: "I don't mind dying. I just don't want to be
there when it happens." He used to say, "You know, he almost had
it there." What was missing? I think of the old saying – "To gain a
certain thing, you must become a certain person, but once you become that person you may no longer need to gain that thing." In short,
Woody could joke about it but what about "living" it?

Death is at the core of Zen because it is at the core of life.
Hakuin wrote about the terrific virtue of what he called, "The great
death," his version of Dogen's "Dropping body and mind; mind and
body dropped." It is liberation itself he is referencing, the realization
of samsara, this world as created by a wandering inattentive mind,
AS nirvana, the great perfection of vast wisdom, compassion, and
non-self-centeredness. He is speaking about seeing through avidya
– a Sanskrit word meaning primal ignorance of our non-dual nature.
Hakuin is talking about dying to all that and all that rises from it. (An
introductory koan which students work on after an initial koan like
"Mu" or the "Sound of a Single Hand" says, "Get out of a locked dun-
geon." You must demonstrate the solution.) The Buddha's teaching is
traditionally known as a poison drum. Anyone who hears it is killed
dead. Isn't that great news?!

It's not just an Eastern thing. In 1826 in London, William Blake
signed a guest book with a beautiful drawing of a human figure
stretched out as if reclining or flying. Surrounding this elegant form
were the words – "William Blake who is very much delighted in being
in good company. Born November 28, 1757 in London and has died

several times since." I wonder what the other guests at that gathering made of that. Interestingly, in Japan in 1749, Zen Master Hakuin wrote on the occasion of honoring a friend and student who had died:

Turning my head a soaring Mount Fuji capped with snow,
Its lower half flushed in the crimson glow of the rising sun.

Hakuin's heir, Torei, annotated this by writing, "These are lines whose point is grasped after you have died two or three times."

In reality we are dying all the time. We call this ongoing daily, minute-by-minute entrustment to reality "our life." The Rolling Stones' song "Ruby Tuesday" always struck me as charmingly profound with its line, "Dying all the time, lose your dreams and you will lose your mind. Ain't life unkind." Losing your mind unkind? Maybe we should be shouting, "Hooray!" instead.

For the Buddha, death was the activity of his complete entrance into nirvana or his *pari-nirvana*. It was total entrustment, a complete giving into the actuality of realization. Practice-realization itself is an entrustment, which Dogen says releases birds to the sky, flowers to spring, snow to the winter, us to ourselves. It is the sustained exertion or continuous practice of this moment, allowing everything to fully *Be*, without attempting to force it into accord with our cherished hopes and expectations.

When we release our clinging, and accommodate reality *as it is*, the ten thousand things can step in and *be* us, which, as Dogen says is intimacy or realization. Such dying is the essence of fullest living. Breath by breath we entrust ourselves to the universe, to the elements that brought us forth, to our own thoughts and deeds, to our ancestors, loved ones, planet, and children. To the "mysterious affinities" of our karma. It is the Way of ripeness and completion. The morning of the Buddha's great realization, the Morning Star stepped in and realized itself as Buddha.

And yet...when death says, "Ready or not – here I come," while intellectually we have always known this was coming, accepting that *the moment* has arrived can be very hard. Remarkably, Zen masters of old seemed to have found a way to enter their final moments without reservation. Some died seated, some standing, some standing on their heads, some giving teisho, some eating cake or writing a poem, some with a great laugh or shout. One old timer groaning in pain indicated that his groans were themselves a kind of prayer or praise – make of that what you will. Contemporary teachers, too, have ended their days on a note of humor or calm. Practicing sincerely, we may also uncover the essence of the liberating insight that brought relief from our mortal terrors.

The impermanence unto death of our own cherished self is the source of our greatest anguish and, as such, also underlies all acts of foolishness and evil. We can be so terrified of impermanence that in seeking to protect our precious, yet, fading self we strike out, causing endless harm. That news is writ large these days. Perhaps it was always so.

In light of this, the Buddha aimed his teaching at one target only – ending suffering – the unnecessary pain we cause ourselves and others, due to avidya – fundamental ignorance of our own nature. A Buddhist parable relates that the great teacher was once sitting with his community (or sangha) in a grove of trees, where countless fallen leaves littered the ground. He asked, "Are there many or few fallen leaves?" "Many, Honored One," his sangha dutifully answered. The Buddha then held up a handful of leaves. "And, now, many or few?" "Very few," they answered. He said, "While the knowledge I have gained through enlightenment is like the many leaves, what I teach is only this handful. For I teach one thing only – the ending of suffering."

The Buddha also said, "Imagine someone who's been struck by an arrow. The physician arrives but before the wounded person will permit the doctor to remove the arrow and treat the wound, they ask, 'Tell me. Was I shot with a claw-headed arrow or one with a straight point? Is the shaft spiral feathered or not? Was the shooter left- or right-handed?' Such a person," said the Buddha, "would die before the arrow could be removed."

The arrow of impermanence has already struck each one of us. How shall we respond? How will we be healed? The essential point is to remove the arrow and get well. But will we? The point of practice is not to think about doing it, but to do it. Which means steadily, with consistency, committing ourselves daily to the count, the breath, the koan.

February 16th marks the date on the Mahayana calendar of the Buddha's entrance into nirvana. How did the Buddha make his transition from this life? The word "nirvana" literally means "blown out," the way a candle's flame is blown out by the wind or a breath. *Poof!* Gone. Nirvana is the blowing out of all lingering flames of greed, anger, self-centeredness, and ignorance. What remains when even the faintest traces of ingrained, self-centeredness are gone, gone, entirely gone? For a realized Buddha, the passage is said to mark yet another step on the unfathomable road of complete fulfillment. Prajna-paramita, perfect wisdom, is "gone beyond" knowledge. More immediate than thought, it splits the sky like a lightning bolt, scores the night like a shooting star.

Dogen says that mature, selfless practice continues endlessly. Practice doesn't end with something called, "realization" or "enlightenment." Rather, practice-realization is renewed and matures endlessly. While the *essence* of practice-realization is the same for beginners as for Buddhas, the *actualization* of practice evolves. Intimacy with counting the breath, with each breath, with a koan is "going beyond" dualistic views of "me in here, everyone and everything else out there." There is no longer room for *this* relative *to* that. Focusing on the practice, the relative world and the self that maintains it are momentarily "gone, gone, entirely gone." This dying is prajna-paramita, perfect, non-dual Wisdom, which carries with it the flavor of nirvana. Doubt in Zen, is not skepticism but a willingness to face questions that no one can answer for us, no teacher, and no Buddha: "Why was I born, why must I die? Why is there injustice? Who is it that right now hears with these ears, sees colors with these eyes?" Doubt is faith in action. In "Dharma Nature," section 23 of his *Shobogenzo, Eye of the Treasury of the True Dharma*, Dogen writes,

> Grass, trees, and forests are impermanent; they are buddha nature. Humans, things, body, and mind are impermanent; they are buddha nature. Land, mountains, and rivers are impermanent, as they are buddha nature. Unsurpassable, complete enlightenment is impermanent, as it is buddha nature. Great pari-nirvana is buddha nature, as it is impermanence."
> – *Treasury of the True Dharma Eye: Zen Master Dogen's Shobo Genzo*, ed. by Kazuaki Tanahashi

As for impermanence, we have this in our koan curriculum, *Blue Cliff Record*, Case 29:

> A monk asked Tai Sui (Daizui), "When the conflagration at the end of the kalpa sweeps through and the great cosmos is destroyed, I wonder, is this one

destroyed or not?"

Daizui said, "It will be destroyed."

The monk said, "Will it be gone with everything else?"

Daizui said, "It will be gone with everything else."

This can be taken as a Zen Buddhist version of tough love. But it can also be seen as a tender gift. When the compulsive, habitual addiction to "me and my" falls away, when it is blown out like a candle's flame, what then is there?

Dogen writes,

> What is the one thing that bodhisattvas guard? It is the aspiration for enlightenment. Bodhisattvas, great beings, always endeavor to guard this aspiration for enlightenment just as people in the world protect their only child. It is like a one-eyed person protecting the working eye, or people traveling in a vast wilderness protecting their guide. Bodhisattvas guard the aspiration for enlightenment in this way. Because bodhisattvas guard the aspiration for enlightenment, they attain unsurpassable, complete enlightenment. Because bodhisattvas attain unsurpassable, complete enlightenment, they embody consistency, enjoyment, freedom, and purity. This is unsurpassable great parinirvana.
>
> – *Treasury of the True Dharma Eye: Zen Master Dogen's Shobo Genzo*. Tanahashi, *section 70, "Arousing the Aspiration for Enlightenment"*

World ages ago, countless lifetimes back, the Buddha was said to have been an ordinary person who one day awoke to a felt need for Truth. After that he worked at it, sometimes in happy, sometimes in difficult or challenging circumstances. Buddhist tradition says that was only after lifetimes of such effort, countless failures and triumphs, that, 2500 years ago he at last awoke fully, as the ex-prince Siddhartha Gautama, thereby becoming the realized Buddha, Shakyamuni. Then, from the foundation of that profound realization, for the next fifty years until his death at eighty he taught others how to also realize the same liberating Truth. Dying all the time, breath-by-breath living, it turns out, is itself the unsurpassable great pari-nirvana. The Buddha's teaching is what he *does*. How he lives, is how he guides us. It is all of a piece, like a single length of unstained silk.

The model and the challenge that the Buddha's life offers, stands before us. In our own Zen life of Buddha we, too, can't simply talk about understanding, like I'm doing here. Ultimately, we are called forth, each one of us, to demonstrate whatever understanding we might have or might not have, and not just in the formalities of a dokusan room before a transmitted teacher. This is something we will each face at moments in our own living and dying whether we've realized a thing, whether we're even practicing or not.

This is our life and, each moment of it is its final ending as well as, simultaneously, its new beginning. If you want to know where you might enter Zen and where you will find your own Zen life of Buddha, why not enter *here*?

About the author

RAFE JNAN MARTIN, founding teacher of Endless Path Zendo, Rochester, New York is a lay Zen teacher in the Harada-Yasutani koan line. A personal disciple of Roshi Philip Kapleau (*Three Pillars of Zen*) and the editor of Roshi Kapleau's final books, he also trained with Robert Aitken Roshi (Diamond Sangha) and, later, with Danan Henry Roshi, founder of the Zen Center of Denver both a Kapleau lineage teacher and a Diamond Sangha Dharma Master. In 2009 Rafe received lay ordination and, in 2016, *inka*, or formal certification of his successful completion of the Diamond Sangha koan curriculum, as well as Dharma transmission, or authorization to teach as an independent Zen teacher.

Rafe is also an award-winning author of over twenty books and an internationally known storyteller whose work has been cited in *Time*, *Newsweek*, the *New York Times*, and *USA Today*. He is a recipient of the prestigious Empire State Award for the body of his work. His most recent books are *Before Buddha Was Buddha: Learning from the Jataka Tales*, (Wisdom Publications, 2017), *The Buddha's Birth* (Merlinwood Books, 2022) and *The Brave Little Parrot* (Wisdom, 2023).

He has spoken at Zen and Dharma Centers around the US and in Canada, and his writings have appeared in *Buddhadharma*, *Tricycle*, *Lion's Roar*, *The Sun*, *Parabola*, *Zen Bow*, *Enquiring Mind*, and other noted publications.

www.endlesspathzendo.org and www.rafemartin.com.

Bibliography

Centuries, Poems, and Thanksgivings. Thomas Traherne. Edited by H.M. Margoliouth. Oxford Clarendon Press. 1958

Complete Poison Blossoms from a Thicket of Thorn: The Zen Records of Hakuin Zenji. Translated by Norman Waddell. Counterpoint. 2017

Crossing the Yellow River: Three Hundred Poems from the Chinese. Translated by Sam Hamill. BOA Editions. 2000

Irish Fairy Tales. James Stephens. Macmillan. 1968

The Blue Cliff Record. Translated by Thomas Cleary and J.C. Cleary. Foreword by Taizan Maeuzumi Roshi. Shambhala. 1992

The Gateless Barrier: The Wu-men Kuan (Mumonkan). Translated and with a Commentary by Robert Aitken. Northpoint Press. 1990

The Lord of the Rings (3 vols.) J.R.R. Tolkien. Houghton Mifflin. 14th printing.

The Poetry and Prose of William Blake. Edited by David V. Erdman. Commentary by Harold Bloom. Doubleday 1965

The Three Pillars of Zen. Roshi Philip Kapleau. Doubleday. 1989

Treasury of the True Dharma Eye: Zen Master Dogen's Shobo Genzo. Edited by Kazuaki Tanahashi. Shambhala. 2010

What? 108 Zen Poems. Ko Un. Foreword by Allen Ginsberg. Introduction by Thich Nhat Hanh. Translated by Young-moo Kim and Brother Anthony of Taize. Parallax Press. 2008